TERRAIN

TERRAIN

Poems

by Gina Hietpas

**BLUE CACTUS
PRESS**

Blue Cactus Press | Tacoma, Washington

This book is dedicated to JTB and VFB

and all families who have made the courageous choice of organ donation. You have given us the gift of many years together.

CONTENTS

Coyote Speaks to Me

So you want to know this place? Be up at dawn,
when first light brushes the sky beyond the grove
of madrones you call the seven sisters.

Don't whine. Learn by exposing yourself
to the dark and cold.
I sleep in the blackberry tangle edging the hayfield,
my thorn fortress warmed by southern light.

Every fall, glossy fruit hangs outside my door. Breakfast.
There's the pioneer orchard, trees gnarled,
apples like knobs, but I tell you – nothing like a feast
of field mice and fallen apples.

It's a quick lope along the fence to the ravine.
Good mousing by the cedar posts
bunched with grass and ragged leaves.
Listen. The water, eighty feet below,
roars with yesterday's rain.

Stick with me!
I'll show you persistence and the art of pounce.
Watch me shrug off disappointment.

In solitude you learn your story.
Only then can you riff on the moon.

I Take My Chances with a Seasonal Man

There was a time, your green shirt ripe
with herring roe was pungent comfort.

You, gone again for the salmon run.

Me, city bred, newly wed
plunged into cold water living:
prime the pump, lime the privy, sliver kindling.

I polish the cook stove's blue porcelain door,
such a fine Wedgewood,
tidy the drawers of the kitchen hutch,

first date receipts, errant buttons, string too short to save,
a clutch of mismatched dice.
Shake for luck and roll.

Stuck, I scour the sour whiff of mushrooms,
grey decay crouched in corners.
I must not cower.

Alone. Trim the wicks, light the lamps.
Feed the fire. Listen to coyote chatter.

Riffing on the Moon

A full moon rides the scruffy sky.
Restless as incoming tide, I wander,
room to room, in raw pursuit of sleep.

Led by mosaic light, I step into the yard
to breathe frost and stars
and expanded space.

A coyote yips an opening chord.
The pack jubilates – howling tremolos,
braided barks, a high descant.

Across the valley another band accepts the challenge,
riffs with alto warbles, solo yelps,
a running keen.

Echoing pitches volley, a call and response
of boundaries and bonds.
As the canticle fades, final alpha barks

dissolve all illusion of aloneness.

Coyote Chatter

Let it roll! Odds on such a pair!
Howl, growl, bicker. Yip, yip, yap!
Late night harmonies.

Listen for the snap of shells, the click of chamber load,
distrust the musk of snares, the scent of sentimental.
They call me trickster, hipster, predator, editor.

Here's the truth –
Each day is a Rorschach blot.

The tape deck croons, *Just the Two of Us*.
Take a chance, but remember:
cord the wood, wrap the pipes.

What We Dreamed

An old logger told us about this place
a south sunny knoll, fine break for a boy
lugging sugar sacks to the moonshine still
cached in the ravine.

Luck and meager savings bought us that land,
acres etched with generations of stories
to which we might add our own,
a reprised "go west" dream.

Christmas Eve, drenched in the Milky Way,
we warmed ourselves with possibilities.
We assumed blessing in the winks of stars.

Dessert

After supper,
we abandon the dishes to walk through the orchard.
Choosing a summer apple, you offer first bite.
Dimpled redness breaks to bright flesh,
cider drips through my fingers.

I hand it back. Your teeth fit the ledge
created by mine. Three quick bites
and you flip the core to the cows.

We move on to plums,
golden green oozing nectar, or purple
hiding tart interiors? We alternate,
then think of blackberries in the far field.

Threading through nettles and thorns,
we pick only the plumpest clusters,
ruddy juices stain our lips and fingers.

Saving some for breakfast, we stop to read coyote scat,
appraise our future in the clouds.

Aria: We Are Introduced to Our Future

Fifteen degrees, snow slumps drape
    across the windows.
In the loft, under outer shingles,
    a winter wren fluffs feathers
    warming the air.

You lie awake in sharp-strummed pain,
    still so I can sleep.
I lie awake, white-knuckle still,
    afraid to provoke your pain.
Above us, the winter wren rustles.

Tomorrow, it will perch on an elderberry stalk
    and trill with cascading joy,
    crescendos bursting the air,
in this deep winter, a radiance
    against bleak days.

Tomorrow, your morphine-laced body,
    splayed on steel-edged tables,
    pictured and probed,
will reveal in grainy images the seismic shift
    in our dreams.

Come night, the wren rests above us,
    composing comfort out of air.

Hospital Admission

I.

You're stuck
awaiting injections, projections, analysis, dialysis.
Sirens wail in the street like a southeaster screaming
across the corner of our cabin.
Uremic smells outdo the chickens' coop.

Self-diagnosing my anxiety, I walk out
into the urban forest where magnificence
is measured in the height of steel and glass
instead of layered cambium.

II.

I hear the creek's swollen roar
in the channeled freeway, a cascade
of freight trucks, high-octane cars.

Confined by curbs and stoplights,
pedestrians crowd like chickens
pressed against the fly pen
clamoring for kitchen scraps.

III.

Shops promise forever in faceted stones,
such bright window dreams.
I have an emerald ring, authoritative swirls
and matriarchal heft. Could it make me urbane?

It fits my finger, but not my frame.
I need a wizard's ring, a sapphire laser to bewitch reality.
I need the feel of one warm, fresh laid egg
in the palm of my hand.

IV.

My body craves the lush displays,
cashmere cocoons to defy the coming chill.
But my hands betray me,

unpolished hands that love dirt and buck hay.
Rough hands aching for the curve
of your calloused palm.

Re–entry

Jays and squirrels siege the walnut tree,
mice mementos litter the kitchen,
raccoons raid the neglected orchard.

In our absence,
the urgency of autumn arrived.

City frayed, we covet sleep,
but a flicker hammers the eaves
insisting otherwise.

All this animal bunkering,
they know the winds have changed.

Unable to even sort the mail,
I watch the jays, undaunted
by the walnuts' brittle husk
and fisted shell.

Everything Is Metaphor

Against time, I wait, home
as your blood is scrubbed three hundred times,
the bulging fistula a kiss between man and machine.
Against the drumming November rain, I wait

for the diesel thrum of the old Rabbit.
You come without greeting, pull me

into the bathroom, close the door,
blocking our son who faints at blood.

Holding your arm over the tub, I tug
the soggy sleeve of the blue and black Filson jacket.
Your arm sprays bright blood across white porcelain,
a river pumped by shivers of shock and cold.

Do not cower! Power pressure the pulsing knot.
Seal! Heal!
Do not cower.
Our son who faints at blood howls,
Open this door!

Coyote Transforms the Blues

My hands rest on raw studs,
the unfinished frame of the west window.
I think of you, your weary body.

In ragged light, coyote trots across our field.
Right before the trees he bounds
onto a gritty patch of snow, prances
into a shaft of late sun –

rears high on hind legs, arches,
twists up and into a dive.
A quick spin explodes a spray of crystals.

He leaps again, lands
precisely on front paws.
Then a half turn, pause,
and a deep bow to my applause.

The spot dims.
He exits into the woods.
Under snow, a mouse trembles.

I breathe
and practice a quick pirouette.

New Year's

I awake to the surprise of snow,
elk bedded down in the outer pasture.
Coaxing the fire back to warmth,
I sit

as day slips into being.
Our son and I bundle up for winter chores –
hay, water, wood. Rhythmic work
broken with snowballs and bursts of chase.

We roll, spin ourselves a chrysalis,
discover wings and stretch wide
into momentary angels longing to leave
a perfect impression.

Shadows lengthen.
The elk move on.
Clad in icicles, we return home
grateful for mittened fingers,

 you waiting by the fire.

Cruising for Chickens

In breaking light, I watch the hens
       clack and scratch awake the day.
I check my chore list, count eggs and obligations.
They focus on feed, beak to business,
       squawk the proper order.

Motionless, I defer to the sun.

A whisk of wings, eagle glides
       above the fuss, cruising for chickens.
Halts the slide, arcs to the tallest tree,
folds into observation.

Eagle watches me
       watching eagle cruising for chickens.

What if I drop these eggs?
What shoulder flick will unleash my wings?
Would I soar for the sun, sear though caution,
lock talons in a spiral plunge?

Would I?

Eagle watches me
       watching eagle cruising for chickens.

Blackberries

Blackberries ripened early this year,
about the time the fevers returned.
Daily, I stand knee deep in brambles
and bounty to pick an offering,
a prayer, an elixir.

On the Occasion of the Twenty–third Surgery

We dance in shadows, you and I,
to jazzy blues, a pharmaceutical beat.
Sway, touch, reverse.
We fly apart, recoil, hold tight.

I master each step in the hospital maze,
ferret out secret halls and stairs,
personal triumph
over the elevators of despair.

I dip in the gloom of *Surgery Waiting*,
glide through the tango of ardent hope.
The silent strain of strangers' pulses –
electronic hustle, jitterbug knees, two step twitches.

We wait, while hearts hips guts are split
wide open, reassembled and finely stitched.
Ruby scars spiral across chests, abdomens, quads.
Signatures of time spent.

We dance with shadows, you and I.
Pain's a cold partner. Embrace me,
lean in. Waltz on.

Raising the Question
  – for JTB

A slant rain weekend,
ocean surge outshouts the wind.

Clutching our coats, we retreat
to a corner table and watch
the violent rollers heave
logs against the bluff
telegraphing thunder beneath our feet.

You order berry pie, no ice cream.
They a piece to share.
For me? Tea.

Truth is, you say, *I'm tired*
Soon I'll be back on dialysis.

He asks, *What can I do?*

Deceptively simple question,
impetus to conversation.
The kind which pries, prods,
pushes to the brink
of action/inaction.

The kind which answers
Who am I?

Consternations

The home nurse asks, *One to ten, how's the pain?*
The answer can be counted in the stack of mysteries
       barricading your chair.
Consternations solved in three hundred pages.

Today, eyeing the numbers, I understand
my conversations must be outside.

The jays squabble over walnut shares,
a ruckus echoed by hummingbirds lusting
       for the last nasturtiums.
You'll want to know flickers have drilled the cedar fence,

coyote stole windfalls from the orchard,
and squirrel stashed his hoard inside the shop.

Because you'll ask, I cross the pasture
and drop into the ravine. Raven's *tonk*
       announces my descent.
Without rain, the creek is depleted to a whisper.

Shivering in the fractured light, I watch
the maple leaves detach, one by one,
       to illuminate my way.

Trapped in Narrative

A bee bumbles on the glassed porch
seeking a clear way out.
Flings against the fixed pane, in furious buzz
until it falls, dazed, on the splintered sill.

The neighboring window flung wide open
admits a sweet jumble – wisteria, lilac,
mock orange, blazing rhododendron nectar.

All that is required is a slight curve of flight.

Walls

The walls in this house are alive.
Cedar, quarter sawn, straight grained
layers of ancient cambium,
and flat sawn
grain that flows like rippled water.

They breathe. Their voice speaks
of seasonal change with creaks or sighs.

The ceiling spruce is spattered with knots,
the floor, birdseye maple, freckled
by a stressful past. Wood rescued
from fire and demolition.

I am enclosed in the bounty of trees.
Secure. And still,

restless. On sleepless nights
I retreat to open air,
lie on the porch and watch
the moon silhouette the droop

of hemlocks' crown, the drape of cedars' limbs
the stiff tiers of fir.

I listen to the branches stir.
Moving air fills my lungs,
soothes my skin, calms
my unruly mind.

Trolling

We launch on choppy waters, row out
through indigo gloom to troll uncertain depths.

What shiny spinner or feathered lure
should dress the hook to drag, a dark bound,
furtive creature gulping into open air?

You offer a speckled lure, and time
to struggle with my knots. I steady myself
against the boat, focus on my hands.

Prevailing winds push us toward an easy drift
in the shallows. Waves chatter against the shore,
and cattails flash vermillion when the blackbird sings.

We tighten against the wind, row back
to deeper waters and cast long.

Morning News

I.

The widow and I seldom speak,
but we are watchful neighbors.
We share yesterday's paper, the prospects for hay,
a common road.

II.

That morning, she tuned–in the news
increased pressure on the border ... another outbreak ...
the ping ping of the black box ...
turned to start the coffee.

The grinder's piercing burr broke beans to dark spice.
She inhaled the smoky promise of routine.
In the stillness, a hoarse groan, her husband gasps for air,
face pressed against cold tiles on the shower floor,
words drowned in harsh blue sucking.

III.

This morning, wakeful, long before the darkest hour,
I see the widow's lights across the road.
Lightly, I lay my hand across your knotted fistula,
amazed by buzz and pulse, blood humming
confirmation.
I match my breath to your chorus of wheeze and whistle
inhale your earthy smells,
move closer.

Ending the Drought

Wind hiss shivers the firs,
sending gusts of moist air through the open window.
The promise of rain tickles
every hair on my arms. Each pore,
parched by a hundred dog days, opens.
My breasts flush, hips soften.

An hour ago, the heat of your persistent hand
was intolerable. Now I slide
my fingers across the fog of sleep,
softly tease your thigh.

South Beach

In the morning, we stretch
  lightly against each other,
align in common warmth,
    the comfort of curves.

All afternoon, we sit
  with unread books watching
gray whales beyond the rollers
    slide in the rise and fall of waves.

Relaxed as breath, they rest
  against the tidal cushion
exposing yards of mottled skin
    submerge, emerge, exhale.

Evening comes, shadows
  consume the whales, the waves.
We linger, bound
    to the pulse of receding tide.

Transformation

Clouds open a steely blue eye,
persistent rain relents.
I walk the tractor path past the pond,
tufted cattails claim the ditches.

Skimming low, an eagle lands
in a curve of rough pasture,
startles up.

... A second, a third follows.
They circle, resettle,

concealed by a swath of uncut hay.

Breathless, I wait
for another flare of flight.

The slap flap of unfurling wings
erupts. An entire convocation rises,
uplift surge shimmies the grass.

Eagles, wing to wing, darken the sky
carrying news
of a mysterious death.

Primal Healing

The breeze cools July heat. Come,
pick blackberries with me, wild trailers
woven across country ditches.
Follow the strands buried in brambles,

lean into the thorns and find ripeness.

Side by side, mostly silent, let's fill
the pierced tin pail, my grandmother's
dented berry grail. We will match
stained hands and nettle sears.

Hoard the moments, tart comfort
for winter days.

The Ache of October

Out of the maple-screened ravine,
a bear dares the expanse of pasture
to gorge on apples, delicious, honey crisp, golden gems
neglected abundance. She layers fat
against dark days.

I, now my mother's age, wrap myself
in russet and gold, sit in the sheen of sun.
Weep. Weep. Murmurs the nuthatch
caching bugs beneath the cherry's bark.

The lawn, radiant with leaves, exudes
the musk of autumn. Inhale.
Breath within the breath
eases the ache of October.

Ghost Elk

I would not have seen the elk
in the autumn flamed thicket
except for the convulsive fly shudder
trembling his flanks.

A ghost bull, completely pale,
his rump patch indistinct
from the grizzled tan of his broad back.

The high–defined haunches
that powered his dominance softened,
hardy thigh muscles sag toward stiffened knees.

The trophy rack wielded to defend
a harem of dark–eyed beauties
reaches now to scratch an elusive itch
or shake down apples from a dying orchard.

Turning Back

Winter consumed six cords of wood,
icicles reached from eaves to earth,
crystal bars across the windows.
What delight to be trapped
in each other's arms!

The night the water barrel burst,
soaking the bed, freezing our boots to the floor,
we laughed
and held each other before the fire
warming first one side and then the other.

Now, the house is weathertight,
decades tamp our conversation.
We embrace
beneath electric heat. Your skilled hands

chamfer my raw edges until we fit again.

Credo

Love is a stone.

It can fracture under pressure.
But yielding to wind or wave,
the sharp edges smooth.

With the right twist,
it skims the surface of unsettled seas,
then sinks to be an anchor.

It is gravel singing counterpoint
to tidal change,
the canyon's whistle against the storm.

Grain by grain, it gives of itself
to become the grit beneath your feet.

Acknowledgements

These poems have had a long evolution with wonderful mentors along the way.

Thank you to Susan Blackaby for inviting me to *Poets on the Coast* with Kelli Russell Agodon and Susan Rich. That was the beginning of believing I had something to share.

Holly Hughes, Tim McNulty, Kate Reavey and my *Last Wednesday* writing group have been steady sources of encouragement.

And special gratitude to Alice Derry for the line–by–line critique which strengthened my skills and refined the manuscript.

You all are a vital part of this work.

The opening poem in this collection was first published as "Coyote Talks to Me" in *Minerva Rising*; "New Year's" was published in the *Poesia Series, Lost Mountain Wincry* (1995); "Riffing on the Moon" was published in *Tidepools* (2019); "Dessert" appeared in *Spindrift* and *Last Wednesday Anthology* (2019); "Credo" appeared in *New Plains Review* and *Last Wednesday Anthology* (2019); "Blackberries," "Walls," "What We Dreamed," "Transformation," and "Ache of October" were all published in *Last Wednesday Anthology* (2019).

About the Author

Gina Hietpas is a self-taught poet, born and raised in Tacoma, Washington. Nowadays, she lives outside Sequim, Washington, on a small farm with her husband, a few cows and a passel of chickens. Her land is a habitat for elk, deer, coyotes and an occasional bear. It is, for the most part, a peaceful coexistence. Several seasons as a backcountry ranger for Olympic National Park shaped her deep connection to wilderness. She has worked professionally as the director of a non-profit and a middle school teacher. Now that she has retired, she focuses her efforts on writing. She has studied with Kelli Russell Agodon, Alice Derry, Holly Hughes, Susan Rich and Kim Stafford. Hietpas' work has appeared in *Minerva Rising, Tidepools, Spindrift* and *New Plains Review*.

Blue Cactus Press is a micro-publisher based in Tacoma, Washington.

We craft books that inspire dialogue about the undercurrents of humanity. We're particularly interested in poetry, short-stories and essays that shed light on the under-currents of our shared human experience. Visit us online at bluecactuspress.com.

Other Poetry Book Published by Blue Cactus Press:

The Art of Naming Your Pain by Kellie Richardson

Low Static Rage by Michael Haeflinger

Still Clutching Maps by Christina Butcher

There Must Be More Than This by Lux Barker / *How to Overstay Your Welcome* by Christina Butcher (Chapbook Series, Summer 2018)

What Us Is by Kellie Richardson

Forthcoming Poetry Books:

Green River Valley by Robert Lashley